Youth In Asia by Allen

Though based on historical events, this is a work of fiction. The main characters are fictional. Any similarity to actual people is purely coincidental.

For any additional information about this book, upcoming books, or to contact the author, please go to WWW.ALLENTIFFANY.COM

At least half of earnings will be donated to organizations that support our wounded veterans. Information on the donations will be posted on my web site on the anniversary of the first edition publication.

First Edition: March 2015
Second Edition: April 2015 (Corrected three minor typos in the paperback version)
Third Edition: July 2015 (Added map, corrected two minor typos in the paperback version)

Early Praise for Youth In Asia

★★★★★

...a very realistic and at times, a disturbing rendering of the war in Vietnam...a great story...

Dennis Waller **TOP 500 REVIEWER**. June, 2015

★★★★★

This is not the stuff of hero's (although there will be heroics), this is the stuff of real men of war and the ravages that they will face...

William D. Curnutt **TOP 1000 REVIEWER VINE VOICE**, June, 2015

★★★★★

I rank it with "Better Times than These", "The 13thy Valley" and "Sand in the Wind" as some of the best fiction to come out of the war.

James W. Durney **TOP 1000 REVIEWER VINE VOICE**, June, 2015

Youth In Asia

Contents

To Pay a Debt

I would like to acknowledge a group of people to whom I – and many of us – owe a large debt. Though I did not serve in Vietnam, I was trained – both as a soldier and as a young leader – by the officers and soldiers who did serve there and remained in service after the war to help rebuild the Army. They are a special breed.

These men and women rebuilt America's military after it was shattered by the Vietnam War and events in America between about 1968 and 1974. In that timeframe, America was a place of contradictions, confusion, and great turmoil. Leaders were assassinated, Martin Luther King and others fought for the rights of all Americans, woman asserted their status as equal to men in jobs and sexual freedom, marijuana was widely available and cool, and a new kind of music with a much harder, angry edge was growing in popularity. Additionally, Americans were becoming much more affluent, with televisions in almost every home.

Our government, though, was losing its ability to form and control public opinion as the evening news showed events as they happened, which was unprecedented, and seemed at odds to what we were being told. Our leaders had come of age molded by the Great Depression and their experiences in WWII, which was a fight that was tremendously challenging but easily understood. As a result, they'd become disconnected and reactionary, desperate in their attempts to remain in control. They lost their ability to lead the country. President Nixon resigned shortly before he could be impeached for criminal acts.

Concurrently, America conscripted young people against their will to spend years in the military. We kept half a million men and women in an Asian country most Americans could not find on a map, to fight a war by self-imposed rules that the other side would not abide. And we had no clear understanding of what outcome we desired or how to achieve it. After 1968, that lack of vision led to years of slaughter on both sides, and a military disintegrating from confusion, loss of discipline, and increasing drug and alcohol abuse.

In the midst of this, a cadre of young officers like Colin Powell, Norman Schwarzkopf, and likeminded men and women in the military, and associated civilians held together the Army, Navy, Air Force, and Marines. They did so by sheer force of will, integrity, and an unyielding conviction that they could help rebuild these organizations while also caring for our young men and women in uniform.

I saw these great leaders in action. These troops raised me in a professional sense. I will be forever in their debt.

So this one is for our troops, which is why half of the money I earn from the sales of this novella will go to organizations that help our wounded veterans. It is a small thing I can do to help mitigate their pain and sacrifices and to help repay what our Vietnam Veterans have given me.

A. L. Tiffany

Map of The Central Highlands

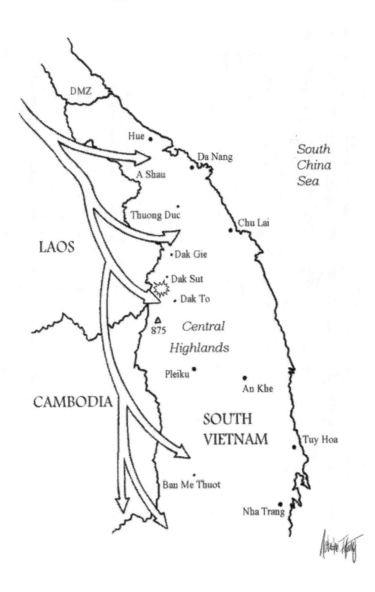

Part 1: The Letter

Liam,

You never asked me to tell you about my short time in Vietnam, but your mom tells me you'd like to hear some of it. She also said you're thinking about joining the Army, so I thought I'd tell you. But I wanted to tell you the whole story, in context.

Now that I'm retired and your grandmother has passed on, I'm not so busy, so I wrote out what happened—the one incident, and one person, I still think about. I wrote this last year, not sure what I'd do with it. I just needed to write it out before it's too late for me.

Honestly, it's been damn lonely. I never thought retiring could be so miserable. And since your grandmother died, it's as if my life's purpose is gone. I still have your mom and you, but you're in California now, and my back hurts too much to sit in an airplane seat for so long. Yes, I have money and a nice house, but I hate all of it. I'm sitting around waiting for Alzheimer's to set in, or to have a stroke, I guess.

Before you enlist, you should read a book called *We were Soldiers Once … and Young*, about one of the big, early battles in Vietnam. The first time I saw it, I thought it was the stupidest book title I'd ever seen. I'll tell you, though, now I think it's one of the most insightful titles and books about soldiers ever written. Once we *were* soldiers. And once we *were* young. It probably doesn't make any sense to you now, but if you do join the Army, it will someday.

When I wrote out my story last year, I tried to write it pretty much as it happened. I figured that would be the best way to make it realistic. I think reading it will help you understand what it all meant. You don't have to respond or say anything. In fact, don't. I just thought I'd share it with someone. I never told my wife this story, at least not the details. It's a cliché, but time goes by too fast. I was going to tell her someday, but I waited too long, so I'm telling you now.

I was not in Vietnam for very long. I left shortly before the Tet Offensive—"Tet" is "New Year" in Vietnamese—in 1968. While I was there, I did what I had to do. I wish things had been different. I tried to keep my team alive. If you do enlist and move up the ranks, you'll think the same things one day.

Grands

Part 2: The Central Highlands

In November 1967, the 173rd Airborne Brigade took Hill 875, near Dak To, in what we called the Central Highlands of South Vietnam. The 173rd drove a North Vietnamese Army division back into Cambodia. This foreshadowed the slaughter that came in January: the Tet Offensive of 1968.

What happened on and around Hill 875 was a victory, we said. But the Airborne Brigade had lost almost two hundred men. Another 642 were wounded during the battles for Hill 875 and the area around Dak To. Though the NVA's bigger formations fled across the border, the 173rd had to keep up the pressure so the enemy couldn't regroup and return. To do so, the bloodied brigade was loading up with replacements.

I arrived in Vietnam in mid-November. I came from the Second Infantry Division in Korea, where I'd been patrolling the demilitarized zone. I'd hoped the Army would send me back to the States after my year in Korea, but with things really heating up in Vietnam, I got orders to go there instead. At the time, I figured a year in Vietnam wouldn't be too bad. I had a year and a half left on my enlistment, and I wanted to go to college when I got out. At the time, I dreamed of being a teacher. I thought I had something to offer others.

I thought the occasional short firefights with the North Koreans, when I patrolled the DMZ, had prepared me for Vietnam. I quickly realized that what I had seen in the DMZ was nothing like the firefights I would soon see in the Central Highlands. But at the time I was confident in my ability as a soldier. Vietnam hadn't started to get weird, so it didn't intimidate me. I wasn't happy about more time overseas, but I figured I could deal with it just as well as sweating out another year in Fort Polk or Hood or some other hole. I was twenty and not in much of a hurry.

When I completed my infantry training at Fort Benning, I'd then gone to airborne school because I had orders to go to the 82nd. The Army, though, changed its mind and rerouted me to Korea.

Because I was jump qualified, I got orders to the 173rd when I got to Vietnam—not that there were many airborne operations there. But who knows how the Army thinks.

After arriving, I spent a week in-processing near Saigon. Then I spent another week at a MACV (Military Assistance Command, Vietnam) school with two hundred other new soldiers, including a couple from Australia. The MACV instructors taught us about the climate, the vegetation, the animals and insects, and the Vietnamese people and their history. We had a few hours of language training and learned some basic words and phrases.

Then we had classes on the enemy, how the Viet Cong and the North Vietnamese Army operated. They taught us about operational security. We learned the enemy was adept at using information they took off dead GIs, from trash Americans left behind, and from listening in on our radio conversations. We heard the story of an American platoon that lost a book of call signs, code words, and frequencies. A day later, an English-speaking Viet Cong soldier got onto their frequency. He directed the platoon of about twenty soldiers into an ambush. Only seven men lived through it.

While going through the in-processing classes, we kept hearing about the fights around Dak To and elsewhere. At night, we'd sit in the barracks and talk about the battles and all the tales the instructors used to scare us. We also combed *Stars and Stripes* and listened to Armed Forces Radio for information and stories about the various units we'd soon join. And I read an article in *Time* detailing General Westmoreland's upbeat presentation to the United States Congress about the war effort.

On the first day of December, they hustled fifteen of us out to Tan Son Nhut airport. The surprisingly cool day was the only thing that entire month to make me think of Christmas. We boarded a C-130 with its propellers already turning. It took us way upcountry, and we stayed in Da Nang overnight. They had us sleep in a hanger with some Marines that were on their way further north, to a small city called Hue that would soon be a slaughterhouse.

The next morning a Huey helicopter flew six of us to the 173rd's basecamp. That long ride flew us over the most gorgeous, green country I've ever seen. It was hard to believe there was a war raging in all that beauty.

The base camp was another story. It was the foulest smelling place I've ever been, but I didn't stay long. I again spent two days doing the in-processing dance before arriving in Bravo Company, 4th Battalion, 503 Airborne Infantry Regiment. They assigned me to Second Squad of Bravo Company's First Platoon.

My squad leader was a black man named Wicker, a high school dropout from Georgia, who smoked nonstop by day. He treated his men well and he knew his shit, as we used to say. We got along well. He didn't have any other prior-service men in his squad, and he was short three men, having only eight of the eleven men authorized, so he was glad to see me. Since I was a corporal, he put me in charge of one of Second Squad's two teams. At the time, the team had four men in it, including me. As a team leader, my job was to do the assigned missions and keep my men alive.

Things went well my first weeks there. We went on four missions. Most were two- or three-day sweeps with long nights lying in ambush. There was little action throughout the battalion's area, but we got into one fight. It was short and vicious. A man in another squad got his face shot off. My team came upon two of the North Vietnamese Army regulars who'd hit us. They tried to run, but I sent two of my men to block them with fire, and when the enemy soldiers switched directions, I was waiting for them. I shot one in the back, and my men hit the other one.

In retrospect, it was a good first fight for me. I found out I could overcome my fear enough to think as well as fight. I suppose letting your men down in combat is every leader's biggest fear. It was mine.

The next morning, after waiting along a trail all night, we found four sets of fresh footprints in the mud in front of us. We were amazed and spooked that enemy soldiers could have stumbled right into us. We'd been in two-man positions, side-by-side so we could sleep in shifts. I guess it's possible we all fell asleep, though that seemed unlikely. You can tell when someone's fallen asleep on watch because you wake up late for yours. That hadn't happened, however. It had been foggy, and we decided later we must have spent so much time watching the gray clouds through the trees, we mistook the enemy soldiers for more of the wispy bands of mist and let them slip by. Like so many other things in war, we never figured it out.

On December 16, we worked out of a battalion firebase on top of a hill. My battalion patrolled the area, looking for the enemy. Our Bravo Company manned the perimeter while the other two companies searched the area.

I watched a big twin-engine helicopter called a Chinook come in with a load of 105mm artillery ammo slung in a big net under its belly. The Chinooks were often used to carry heavy cargo and light artillery pieces into and out of hilltop firebases. Their huge engines blew dust and debris everywhere, which always made us miserable. Between that and their name, we called them Shit Hooks.

After it put the ammo on the ground, it released the net and then drifted to one side to land, an unusual move for a Chinook. As the ramp at its back came down, the flight crew pushed more cargo out of the back, and three new men walked down the ramp. They were halting and confused and wore new uniforms and new gear, including the stuffed rucksacks on their backs. Cherries, we called them. New soldiers. One of them would belong to me.

Evslin. He was tall, muscular, and good-looking with straight, black hair. Like me, he'd volunteered for the Army. Unlike me, Evslin had volunteered for Vietnam.

We immediately renamed him Elvis. Quiet and smart, he seemed like a good guy. Twenty-one years old and from Chicago, he'd already been in college two years. After graduating from Basic Training and Advanced Infantry Training at Fort Benning, he'd stayed there three months working on one of the rifle ranges before getting orders to Vietnam. We were glad to get a guy with that much weapons experience. For one thing, we figured he was a good shot.

I told Elvis what I expected of him and about some of the other men in the platoon. I told him how we operated, and I went over our standing operating procedures. He listened and took notes. He seemed concerned about doing his job and not letting anybody down. I asked him if he had any questions.

"No, Corporal Jacobs," he said. "I think I'm ready."

"Good," I answered. "'Cause we're going to get another mission soon."

He didn't respond other than to watch me closely. I could tell he was nervous. That was okay. I just needed to make sure I had his attention. Though Hollywood would lead you to believe otherwise, most problems with people new to Vietnam happened when they didn't take it seriously enough.

"Okay. Get your ruck and follow me." I led him to one of my team's fighting positions. It was a bunker occupied by a specialist named Harrington. Specialist is a rank between private first class and corporal. The Army makes specialists out of soldiers who are good at soldiering but not good at leading other soldiers, at least not yet. Men like Harrington. "Spec Fours," we called them.

Harrington was a good man. From Idaho, he was a farmer's son, but he said he hated farms. He'd been the acting team leader before I showed up. I liked him and spent my early days in-country talking to Harrington. He was observant and helpful, but he frowned often. Some guys in Vietnam battened down the emotional hatches until their tour ended. When they got back to the world, they'd come back to life. Harrington was one of those men. Either way, I thought he'd help bring Elvis along.

I introduced Elvis to Harrington before returning to my position with one of our platoon's two machine guns. There was nothing else for me to say. Elvis was starting his year. He'd live through it or he wouldn't. Just like me.

I had one of the platoon's two M60 machine guns assigned to me, because both the platoon leader and platoon sergeant had a lot of confidence in me. My team was usually the trail team – the last team in the line – so we needed the big gun.

A machine gun is a funny thing. You can't hit much with it, but its power scares the hell out of the enemy. M16s are much more accurate and fire much faster, but their bullets can't go through a tree trunk, a mud wall, or a termite hill like an M60's can. An M60 is also much louder and has a much brighter muzzle flash. Of course, machine guns always draw the enemy's most intense fire.

No one could pronounce our machine gunner's long Samoan name. In the middle of those eighteen letters were the four letters T-U-S-I. So we called him Tusi. He was also a Spec Four. Tusi was a big, powerful man with dark skin and black eyes. He rarely spoke at all but when he did, we listened. We often saw him smiling. Tusi always saw the funnier side of things. He'd been in another squad as one of our platoon's point men because he was a natural tracker. When our old machine gunner rotated home, they pulled Tusi off point to carry the M60. No one lasts forever on point. Landmines, snipers—you just can't stay alive long on point. And Tusi liked the big gun.

Private Oltin, Tusi's assistant gunner, carried the extra ammo and spare barrel. Oltin was another new addition to the platoon. A draftee, he'd only been in-country for a few weeks longer than I had. He was thin with bright red hair, and he was having a hard time keeping up with all the stuff we carried. We struggled to take him seriously because any time he started getting mad or defensive, he'd take a big gulp of air and hold it in his mouth so he looked as if he were half blowfish. Oltin was always scared and often had the shits when we patrolled.

Tusi and Oltin were always together. They were a strange pair, but they worked well as a team.

After I left Elvis and Harrington's position, I went to the hole I shared with Tusi and his machine gun. Oltin lay curled up behind it in his poncho, asleep. I sat on the edge of the position and twisted so I could slide into the dark hole. Once inside, I took off my helmet and glanced through the firing slot. We were in a new position, but since we were going to abandon the firebase soon, we hadn't bothered to cut the perimeter vegetation back as far as we had at the brigade basecamp.

I looked across the forty meters of red, rocky ground we'd exposed to where the trees and underbrush stood. The terrain there was very mountainous and thickly vegetated, but it was drier than the lowlands. There were plenty of streams in the surrounding valleys, though. The trees were more of the hardwood variety and taller, and there was less undergrowth on the higher ground.

Tusi and Oltin had cut a small shelf into the front of the position. A litter of M16 magazines, fragmentation grenades, smoke grenades, and the clacker all lay there. The clacker was the size of a man's wallet. When squeezed, it generated an electrical charge that traveled down a wire to a Claymore antipersonnel mine.

Claymores are about the size of a hardback book. They have a light-green plastic shell and small metal legs on one of their long sides. C-4, the military's favorite plastic explosive, lines the back of the mine, in which are embedded approximately seven hundred steel ball bearings. The mines are exploded by the clacker's electrical charge or a blasting cap ignited with timefuse. Essentially a huge shotgun shell, when it goes off it shreds everything in its path out to thirty meters.

Each position had at least one Claymore in front of it.

After scanning our sector for several seconds, I leaned against the back wall of the position.

"Anything?" I asked Tusi.

He shook his head.

The big, black machine gun sat on its bipod. From its left side hung 7.62mm brass rounds held together with black links. Tusi, being the diligent and capable soldier he was, stood behind it. He rested his right shoulder against the butt of the weapon and kept his right hand around the pistol grip. Tusi was great. If you told him to do something, he did it. No questions. No checking up on him. I knew I'd never catch him asleep on duty or have to wait for the machine gun in a firefight unless he'd been wounded.

"Wicker's looking for you," Tusi said.

"About?"

"Didn't say. He'll be back."

I picked up the binoculars and used them to scan our sector. The glasses were powerful enough that I spotted a green snake winding its way up a tree trunk. Curious, I wanted to see what it was hunting. After several seconds, I saw a big spider several feet farther up the tree, partially hidden in a bullet hole.

The spider sat perfectly still among the splintered, toothpick-like pieces of wood blown out of the hole. As I watched, the snake continued to close on the spider. I remember thinking the spider should've tried to get away. Instead, it just sat there. I wondered if it thought the snake would ignore it.

As I expected, I saw a flash of movement as the snake's jaws closed on the spider. The spider's black legs stuck out the sides of the snake's mouth, slapping back and forth though it was too late. The snake did not chew the spider. With the spider's legs still wiggling from its mouth, it turned and made its way down the trunk to disappear into the shadows.

"Corporal Jacobs?"

"Yeah?" I answered, lowering the binos and turning toward the back of the position so I could see Sergeant Wicker.

"Patrol's out effective 1830 to 1915. Stand-to 1920 to 2020."

That was all Wicker said. He rarely spoke much. For the short time I knew him in Vietnam, he was always serious. I respected him for that, and I knew he was thinking hard about how to keep us alive. I don't know if he'd always been so focused or if it was because of what had happened to the squad in November. Of the ten men who'd been in the squad when November started, only four men remained. Tusi and Harrington were two of the four. Three had died on Hill 875, and three had been evacuated for wounds. They never found the foot of one of the guys who lived. He shipped back to the States with no left leg.

The patrol Wicker had mentioned was about to circle the firebase, three hundred meters into the woods starting at 1830. The squad-sized patrol would search for any sign the NVA or Viet Cong were sneaking up on the firebase in preparation for an after-dark attack. Such patrols went out just before sundown and just after sunup every day. While the patrols were out, we'd pull the charge-generating clackers off the Claymores. We feared one of the new soldiers would be so nervous, he'd mistake the sounds a patrol made for the enemy and squeeze his clacker, setting off a Claymore. Once that happened, everyone would start shooting even without a target, and our patrol would be slaughtered by their fellow soldiers.

Like the twice-a-day patrols, we also did stand-to every morning and night. Stand-to started thirty minutes before sundown or sunup and lasted until thirty minutes after, when historically most attacks occur. During stand-to, we'd put every available man on the perimeter. We'd ready every weapon to fire and hang clackers off the ends of the wires leading to the Claymores.

At 1815 hours, I headed to Elvis and Harrington's position. I could hear them talking as I walked up.

"What's that?" Harrington asked.

"A playwright?"

"Yeah."

"A guy who writes plays," Elvis said.

"Why you want to do that? Is that what you were studying?"

"Yeah. Well ... sort of. I was just getting started."

I could tell how excited Elvis was about what he wanted to do. But I figured that like most young men, before they fully believe in themselves, he felt embarrassed to let out the truth and reveal just how desperately he wanted to succeed.

I switched my M16 from my right hand, where I habitually carried it, to my left. I pressed the big knife I carried on my right hip to my thigh to keep it out of the way while I slid to my knees behind their position. I wanted to hear more.

"So why do you want to do that? I mean, you get paid or something?"

"I hope so."

After waiting for a moment, I rolled my wrist and saw it was getting close to 1830. I was about to get up when Harrington persisted, asking, "So tell me, man, how come you want to do that?"

"I ... I think it's ... it's important," Elvis stammered. "Things need to be said, and that's the best way to do it."

He continued, speaking faster. "See, I don't think you can lecture people any more. You have to say things in a way that entertains people, you know? That way I think you can still talk about important things."

"So what are you doing here? How come you're not on Wall Street or something?"

"Broadway ..."

"Whatever."

After a silent moment, Elvis said, "You ever see 'Star Trek'? It's a—"
"The space show with that pointy-eared freak?"

"Yeah, yeah! That's it. You ever hear the beginning? It starts with William Shatner saying, 'Space: the final frontier ...'"

"Yeah, I heard it."

"See, I think he's wrong. I think violence is the final frontier. It will always be the final frontier."

There was a pause. Then, "What? You mean like war?"

"Yeah! Exactly! Lots of famous writers were soldiers or sailors, see? Like Conrad and Hemingway and Mailer ... and they learned—"

"Oh, man. Don't tell me this is your idea of some kind of fucking field trip. You think this war is for you to get ideas or characters or whatever? God damn it."

I heard Harrington kicking the dirt wall of his position before going on. "You stupid fuck. Man ...

I've been here for nine fucking months, okay? I got ninety-two and a wake-up, then I'm out of this slaughterhouse. And I can tell you, the shit here is going to get worse. I can just feel it. We're right here up against Cambodia and Laos with fucking NVA running back and forth over the border and Viet Cong all over the fucking place. You want war? You should've been at Dak To and 875. You don't know shit, cherry. You think this is some kind of bullshit game?"

Elvis said nothing. I started to feel sorry for him, but I was glad Harrington said what he did. Though I sympathized with Elvis, I didn't think he understood the finality of Vietnam, of war, of losing your arms or legs or breaking your back falling out of a helicopter. What death really meant. I wanted to hear more, but I couldn't wait any longer. It was almost 1830.

"Harrington?" I said.

"Yeah?"

I saw his white face in the shadows and gloom of the position, and I smelled the insect repellent he wore. I told him about the patrol and stand-to and waited while he pulled the clacker off the line. "Romeo here thinks he's in Vietnam to do a class study," he said.

"I heard."

"All?"

"Enough." Louder, I called, "Elvis?"

He turned so I could see his face. "Yes, corporal?"

"You got one job over here: Pay attention and do what you're told to do. Otherwise, you won't live long enough to write shit. Is that clear?"

"Yes, corporal."

I stared at him for a few seconds, hoping he'd take to heart what I'd told him.

"They firin' H and I tonight?" Harrington asked.

"Probably. Don't know what time."

"What's H and I?" Elvis asked after a moment.

I turned to look at the skyward-pointing barrels of the six 105mm artillery guns clustered in the center of the firebase. Their dark barrels stuck up above the green sandbag berms we'd built around each gun.

Harrington answered our new man, his voice caustic. "Harassment and Interdiction. Our artillery fires on known and suspected enemy locations. We try to kill them. They try to kill us. It's what we do here. This ain't no fucking play."

Part 3: The Diary

A light rain started at about 0330. I was on duty beside the machine gun. Tusi and Oltin had curled up behind the position in their ponchos. Because there were three of us assigned there, we were doing ninety minutes on and three hours off, so it was better than being in a two-man position.

The nights were oppressive. We had to stay awake, be silent, and not smoke while we were on the perimeter. We weren't supposed to move around or make any noise. Since my life and my men's lives depended on my vigilance, I would do almost anything to stay awake. I would eat the instant coffee out of my C-Ration or do push-ups if that was what it took to remain alert.

I spent my shift scanning my team's sector with the night scope. It needed ambient light to function, and there wasn't much because of the overcast that night. In the green image, I could see little more than the up-and-down lines of the trees and the horizontal line of the ground where we'd cut back the undergrowth.

I heard movement behind our positions and metal tapping against metal. The cannon cockers opened the breaches of their howitzers and began shoving high explosive rounds into the steel chambers. Then there were several minutes of silence before all six guns roared. The flashes of white lit up the trees in front of me. I closed my eyes and looked down to preserve their adjustment to the darkness.

Everyone in the perimeter woke up at the explosions. It happened almost every night. We'd wake up, instinctively take a deep breath, grab our weapons, and spend half a second trying to decide if it was incoming or outgoing. Once we figured out we weren't under attack, we'd exhale and itch with sweat and listen to our hearts racing. The artillerymen would finish their fires at about the same time our hearts would slow, and then we'd lie awake, waiting for our next shift because we were too full of adrenaline to sleep.

Tusi quietly rolled into the position after the second outgoing salvo. He stood beside me with his poncho draped over his broad shoulders as I smelled the coppery odor of burnt powder from the outgoing artillery rounds.

"They had to wait till I was off."

"Yeah," I answered as I turned to the no-man's land between the trees and us. Tusi was to relieve me at 0400. Though it was a bit before his shift started, I turned and asked, "You got this? I want to check the other positions."

"Yeah. Seen anything?"

"Not shit."

When I got to the position Harrington and Elvis occupied, I squatted down behind it and whispered, "How's it going?"

Elvis swallowed so hard I could hear it before he said, "Okay. What's wrong?"

"Nothing. Why?"

"I ... I didn't think anybody was to ... to move around at night unless something was wrong."

I slid in beside Elvis. I understood how scared he was. I remembered the first night I'd spent in the DMZ in Korea. That hadn't been half as scary as this was for a new guy. We talked in whispers as the guns continued to boom out rounds behind us. Elvis and I talked for almost thirty minutes. I asked him about college and told him I wanted to teach someday. What I'd said seemed to calm him down. I realized later he'd begun to think of us as friends. In a way, we were. But friendship always came second to staying alive there.

* * *

Our company ran another patrol from that firebase on Christmas Day, 1967. The area was thick with Viet Cong covering the movement of an NVA regiment. We went looking for a fight. Huey helicopters picked us up from our firebase, six at a time, and we roared over the jungle for twenty minutes. When we did come in to land, we were nearly on the border with Cambodia, and the area was expected to be hot. The pilots didn't want to be sitting ducks, so they wouldn't land. We had to jump off the skids as they slowed and got close to the ground, the door gunners swinging their machine guns back and forth, ready to fire, as we dropped to the dirt.

We were all scared at first, especially Elvis, but he quickly caught on to how boring patrolling was. He hadn't yet experienced the brief minutes that become an eternity when you're in a fight. Elvis began to relax. He always did what he was told, though he tended to keep to himself. I figured that was just his way. I thought he was settling into the unit. No one complained about him.

Wicker was nervous as hell those three days. He rarely spoke, but when he did on that mission, half the time he'd say, "This ain't right." Or "I don't like this" or "I ain't doin' 875 again." The same went for my entire chain of command up to the company commander. There is never much talking in the bush. On this mission, there was almost none. Everyone was scared and extremely vigilant.

There was supposed to be an entire NVA regiment in the area, but we never fired a single round. In spite of what we'd feared, the mission turned out to be three days and two nights of nothing other than repeatedly finding fresh footprints. We were clearly being watched and tracked, but we didn't see a single enemy soldier.

* * *

A week later, we were out in the bush again. It was like every other operation we'd run out there. Each of the brigade's three battalions had its own area of operation and set up its own hilltop firebase. Each battalion went in with three infantry companies and a battery of six 105s, as well as four small mortars for close-in support.

We came in by helicopter and spent the first day sweating as we cut, dug, and blew a perimeter of gun emplacements and bunkers into the top of a hill. Of course, the enemy knew we were there. That was kind of the point. In our arrogance, we wanted them to start a fight with us. If they did, we had so much firepower we could slaughter them as long as we could hold them for a few minutes, long enough to get the artillery on target. If we could hold them for ten or fifteen minutes and there were enough of them, we could get some of the fast movers – jet aircraft – on station to bring in napalm or conventional bombs.

One company was always on the perimeter, and two were always patrolling, looking for a fight. Same old thing. We were on the perimeter first. Then our turn came to go out. It was to be a four-day, three-night operation. Considering the timing of our past operations in the area, we guessed we'd be the last company in and the whole battalion would pull out upon our return. Our patterns were becoming predictable.

When it was our turn, we left the perimeter as a company, at 0245 in the morning. Our platoon was third—last—in the order of movement. We wore our flak jackets and our web gear, on which we each carried M16 magazines, fragmentation grenades, first-aid pouches, canteens, and a bayonet or a big knife, which I preferred to the bayonet. Some of us also carried smoke grenades. On our backs, we wore our rucksacks. We had stuffed them with more ammo, batteries, our chow, and a green plastic poncho to sleep in.

As it got light, and walking just below the top of a ridge—so we wouldn't be silhouetted and spotted from far away—we twisted around the trees and down toward the low ground near a river winding through the bottom of the valley. It was surprisingly hot and humid for that time of year, and big swarms of insects anticipated our moves. After three hours, we reached the valley's bottom. Our platoon leader got a call from the company commander and, as planned, our platoon stopped moving. The idea was that if the NVA were tracking the company, we could break off and set up an ambush to blow them away when they got close.

Though we were all still very nervous, after an hour it didn't look like anyone was following. So our platoon took off at a ninety-degree angle from the way the company had gone. We began working our way through the flatter ground on the south side of the river.

We moved in single file. Our squad was last in line. My team was last in the squad. Our job was to protect the back of the platoon every time we stopped. If we got word we'd be stopped for an extended time, Tusi would put the M60 down in the center of the trail we were cutting. Oltin would go down on Tusi's left to keep the ammunition flowing to the gun. I'd put Harrington on Tusi's right. He'd fire every time the machine gun paused so we had rounds going out constantly. Elvis's job was to stay between me and the next man in the squad and tell us when the platoon started moving again. That way, since the rest of us were facing backward, we'd know when it was time to pull out and we wouldn't get left behind. While we stopped, I'd wait between the men behind the machine gun and Elvis.

If the enemy did come upon us, we were to fire them up and then give ground as we followed the platoon to safety. Each one of us carried a Claymore mine already rigged with a two-minute-long piece of time fuse and a fuse igniter. If we had someone on our ass, we'd ignite the fuses and drop the Claymores on the trail. Two minutes later, they'd go off and kill everything near them. In effect, we'd made huge fragmentation grenades with a two-minute fuse. We hoped that would persuade anyone chasing us that they had better things to do with their lives.

We continued to operate as a platoon, and we saw nothing except leeches and insects our first three days and two nights. It was very quiet in those isolated areas. Everyone reacted to the lack of contact in different ways. Some of the guys got nervous and began to think we were being outfoxed.

The afternoon of the third day, we paused while the Lieutenant and one of the other squads inspected a couple of old huts we'd stumbled across. We remained where we were as they checked it out. I was on the ground beside Tusi. I alternately watched and listened for signs of the enemy and studied a line of ants marching over a rotting limb. They were small and red. I never saw the beginning or the end of their line.

I found it hard to stay interested in what was going on around me. In the dreary afternoon heat, only our self-discipline and the mosquitoes' nonstop attacks kept us awake.

After about an hour, I got up and crept along the trail we'd been cutting. Precisely defined rays of sunlight filtered down through the branches. Dozens of yellow-and-white butterflies dodged back and forth.

Harrington rested against the base of a large tree. I knelt down beside him and whispered, "How you doin'?"

He looked at me and shrugged before glancing away. His right hand was wrapped around the black plastic pistol grip of his M16. Like all of us, his skin was stained a light-olive color by our days of living in sweat and filth. He had dirt under his fingernails and his hands had small, open sores and scratches from the continuous process of weaving through the vines. And he stank, but so did I.

While I rested beside him, Harrington gently slid out his bayonet and raised it above his head. I was alarmed until I saw what he was watching. A small green-and-brown lizard, progressing in jerky bursts, came around the base of the tree. It sprinted over the roots spreading from the trunk.

Harrington quit breathing as it paused on an exposed root just in front of him. His arm flashed down. The lizard tried to flee. The bayonet cut into the bark and stopped. On the left side of the blade was the back half of the lizard, twitching with its tail whipping around. On the right side, the lizard's front legs pounded as if it could still outrun its death. We watched as the top half dragged itself into the undergrowth to finish dying. Harrington looked at me. He lifted his eyebrows and whispered, "Thought I could get him behind his head."

I smiled. "You're too slow."

"Well ... it's just one more casualty now."

Harrington shrugged and frowned. With the tip of the black bayonet, he flicked the lifeless lower half of the reptile into the bushes. Harrington was getting more fatalistic as every day got him closer to the end of his tour.

I quietly stood and rotated away as he returned to studying the vegetation. I moved farther up the path.

Elvis also sat against the base of a tree. He wore his flak jacket open, like the rest of us, because of the heat. Instead of facing out, though, he was scribbling in a small notebook. His M16 lay on the ground at his side. Elvis looked up, but too late. I had him trapped against the tree. I moved my M16 to my left hand. Dropping to my knees, I drove my right fist into his stomach as hard as I could. His helmet banged against the bark of the tree as I punched the wind out of him. His eyes got big in surprise and he drew up his knees and covered his stomach, grabbing at my fist. Before he could cry out, I lifted my hand and pressed it over his mouth. I hissed, "Make a sound and I'll beat the fuck out of you right here!" I was sure I could do it quietly, and sure he thought so, too.

He struggled to catch his breath and sit up, but he didn't fight me. After a moment, I lifted my hand enough to let him breathe. I rotated to one side and picked up the notebook. I turned it over and wiped away the dirt sticking to it. When I opened it to read what he'd been writing, he made a try at grabbing it. I yanked the notebook out of his reach and knocked his hand away. I looked at him. He stared back for a moment before lowering his eyes.

In his neat handwriting, he'd described our operations and his thoughts about the men in the squad. I was impressed with how much he'd written in the short time he'd been with us, and I realized this was not the first time he'd ignored his duty in favor of writing. I began pulling out pages. No particular pattern dictated which pages I tore loose. When I had three or four sheets in my fist, I stuck it in his face and said, "Eat it."

He raised his eyes to look at me but made no other move.

"Hey, shit-for-brains playwright, you too stupid to know this kind of stuff will get us all killed? Didn't they teach you shit about OPSEC?" He didn't answer. I knew he'd had the same classes on operational security when he'd arrived in-country that I had. "Or maybe you just don't give a fuck about the rest of us and don't care if the dinks get this?"

"Yes, I do."

"You what?"

"Care."

"About who?" Before he could answer, I asked, "Are you as fucked up as you wanna be?"

"I—"

"Shut up. We can't burn it or bury it, so you gotta eat it."

He looked at the wad of paper in my hand. I held it closer to his face. He swallowed hard before reaching for the first sheet. I waited as he ate each page. When he finished, I stood and shoved the notebook into a cargo pocket of my jungle uniform pants.

"Can I have it back later?" he asked in a whisper.

"No. It's going in the burn bin when we get back."

I started away, thought about his question, and realized he still didn't get it. I turned around, bent down, and again got in his face. "You got one mission out here. Pay attention. Or it'll be a very long year. Or a very short one because you'll get your cherry head blown off. I'll put you on point until you're dead or get religion." I wasn't sure whether he was listening or he was thinking about killing me—or what he was thinking at all. After a moment, I whispered, "Now pick up your weapon, turn the fuck around, and keep your eyes open."

* * *

Several days later, at our basecamp, I lay on my cot, looking at the blackness over me. Somewhere above was the sloped ceiling of the big tent in which we slept. The rest of the squad was asleep. I couldn't sleep. I was worried. We'd heard more and more reports of enemy activity, small fights, and ambushes. I still had ten months to go.

It was a quiet night. Outside the tent, I could see the blue glow from the moon's light. Still in my uniform, I tried to roll to my side and felt the poncho liner wrap around my legs and the stuff in my pockets push against my skin. I didn't have to wear my uniform or my boots when I slept, but I did. I hated sleeping in my clothes. But the thought of waking up to a surprise attack with no clothes on bothered me more. A year of sleeping in my uniform was bearable.

I wondered how many people in the world had to sleep in their clothes for fear of being attacked in their sleep. And wore their clothes for days, as we did, until they began to rot and tear apart.

In the world. I meant "The World" back home. I was an American soldier, but I lived in a way the people who directed and paid me did not. I lived in a way they couldn't comprehend or even imagine. In that world, people were dodging the draft and starting anti-war riots, riots that would become massive and increasingly violent after the Tet Offensive. America was about to change. At the time, of course, I didn't know what was coming. None of us did. We were just trying to stay alive. But that night, I kept thinking about things like this. I was becoming angry, and afraid. Our enemy was rolling back and forth across a border we could not cross. They were killing us and then running to a sanctuary we had created for them. It made no sense.

Finally, I kicked out of my poncho liner. I remembered Elvis's diary and pulled it out of my footlocker where I'd hidden it. I'd meant to burn it, but I hadn't gotten around to it. I also grabbed my flashlight and two beers I'd stashed in there. Sneaking out, passing the other men, I glanced at

Elvis. He was sleeping on his side, curled up like a child, and wore only his T-shirt and pants.

I stepped out and made my way to our battalion's mess tent. Like the rest of the basecamp, it was blacked-out, but at least it was a place to sit. I figured no one would be there, and even if I used my flashlight, no one would bother me about it.

I pulled the tab on one of the beers. Though it was warm, it tasted good. I turned on the flashlight but kept the red lens on it. At first, I thumbed through the notebook, reading bits and pieces. Elvis's handwriting was small but neat and very legible.

I remember thinking, as I read, that it was like a sketchbook of short notes. It didn't seem like much more than just observations and descriptions. Parts of it caught my attention. He wrote about the boredom of patrolling, the long hours waiting to die or to kill. Elvis noticed how some guys—he wrote about Harrington—seemed eager to kill, and some men like Tusi didn't seem to differentiate between killing and not. He said Oltin lived in constant fear, that he'd been too afraid to dodge the draft and was now too afraid to overcome the constant diarrhea that plagued him whenever we were in the bush.

The last entry I found was about me. He said I understood killing but didn't enjoy it, and I did it for a different reason. "Like most men," he'd written, "it is easier to kill than to create because that is what men have been doing for eons." I didn't know what that meant.

I finished the first beer. I opened the second and started reading the notebook from the beginning.

It took me an hour to finish it. I turned off the light and looked up. My eyes hurt from reading by the red light. Rubbing the heels of my hands against them, I tried to clear my vision. I kept thinking about what I'd read. I wanted to tell myself it didn't make sense and Elvis must be crazy in his own private way.

As my vision cleared, I realized I saw a shadow on the mosquito netting of the tent. The dark form stood facing me but didn't speak. There was little moonlight and it was at his back, so I couldn't tell who stood watching me.

"What's up?" I asked. There was no answer. After a moment, he turned and started away with his head down and his hands in his pockets. I wanted to call to him but didn't.

When I got back to our squad's tent, I saw that Elvis's cot was empty. I quietly returned his notebook to where I kept it in my footlocker and crawled onto my cot. I wanted to stay awake until he returned, hoping to find out if he'd been the dark figure watching me.

When I awoke the next morning, Elvis and Oltin were both gone. Wicker had sent them out on a work detail. He also told me Brigade wanted our Battalion back in the jungle soon. There were more reports of enemy activity in the area.

Part 4: Shit Hook

In mid-January, we were again in the bush. More missions, again near Cambodia. We were west of Dak To again. On this one, we'd been out for three days. The first night, Alpha Company had slammed into an NVA company. They walked into it shortly before midnight. All hell broke loose in the dark. Alpha company had two dead and nine more injured that they couldn't evacuate until morning. When the light came the enemy was gone, but they found three dead NVA soldiers and more blood trails where they'd dragged off their wounded. The enemy soldiers were from one of the units that had fought us at Hill 875.

Going into our last night, we stopped just before the sun went down. We'd separated from the other units in the battalion, and we were moving by ourselves, just our platoon of about twenty-five men. We'd been circling back to the battalion's firebase, but we were still in the low ground. The dirt was black and spongy from the rotting vegetation, and there was a pungent smell of decomposition. We were to set up a small perimeter and silently wait until the sky was pitch black. Normally, by that time of day we'd be in an ambush position where we'd impatiently wait for the planet to rotate 180 degrees. This time, since we hadn't seen any sign of the enemy in the last few days, our company commander decided we'd move all night. If the NVA were tracking us, we'd surprise them by being somewhere unexpected when the sun came up.

It was hot and humid again, but as the sun went down the sky was beautiful—what little we could see of it between the trees. As we waited, the air cooled, and the heavens turned a darker blue. A few high clouds hung motionless, feathering out at one end. They turned orange and then red as the sky behind them faded to black and we squatted in the mud.

Between watching the jungle around me turn black, I watched the stars emerge and listened to the sounds of insects and animals around us. When I'd been on training exercises in the States, I used to look at the night sky and see an occasional airliner fly over. I'd know that somewhere up there people were talking, having drinks, sharing stories, and feeling excited because they were going somewhere new or home to tell their lovers or families about where they'd been. In Vietnam, there were never any such planes. The only aircraft that high above Vietnam were the occasional B-52s flying out of Cambodia or Thailand or Guam, struggling with their racks of bombs.

Whispering started up the line in front of us. Oltin was beside me. He leaned away to get the message. When he turned toward me, his cheeks were puffed out, and in the last light, I saw the bottom of his red sideburns.

"Scout Platoon got ambushed," he whispered. "One of their teams got overrun. Pass it on."

I was scared. We were operating by ourselves, independently of the other units in the battalion. Here it comes, I thought. First, Alpha Company. Now the Scout Platoon.

An hour after dark we began to move.

Traveling at night is an infuriatingly slow process. Still in our single file, we'd move a few feet and stop, move a few feet and stop. It would go on all night as the point man kept working his way through the vegetation. He'd pick his way around trees and impenetrable tangles of undergrowth. The point man would repeatedly trip and walk into spider webs and would have to endure the seconds in silence as they'd scamper across his face. Everything that stopped the point man stopped the entire column. We averaged only a half-mile an hour at night, about one-third of our daytime speed.

Several times when we stopped, word came back that we'd be at an extended halt. Since we were again the trail team, I'd spread out my men for those stops. I'd just have everyone take a knee and cover to the rear. Everyone was doing well and paying attention since we'd heard the report about the Scout Platoon being ambushed.

Shortly after 2330 we stopped again. Wicker came back to talk. I didn't hear him until he was almost on me. One of Wicker's best attributes—one of many—was that he worked hard to keep us all informed about what was going on.

"This is gonna be a long halt," he whispered close to my face.

"What's up?"

"New orders. We're going a new way. Lieutenant is working up a course."

"Enemy?"

"Yeah. Charlie Company came across a cache of ammo and rice. Fresh. We're supposed to change directions so we can sweep the area at sunup."

When he had nothing else to say I asked, "What the fuck happened to the Scouts? They're supposed to be smarter than that."

"Don't know. You heard what I heard. Everybody's luck runs out, so stay alert."

We were a million miles from home playing a deadly game of cat-and-mouse in a black jungle, and it was getting harder to even remember why we were there. When we roared in on our helicopters in daylight, with fast movers ripping over us, protecting us, I felt like the hunter. Now I felt like the hunted. Stay alert.

Wicker put his hand on my shoulder and stood before turning and heading toward the front of the squad. After he left, I wanted to go around and inform my men. But though I don't remember being scared, my right leg started shaking. My right calf muscle began twitching and I couldn't stop it. I had to kneel there and massage it for a few minutes as I listened to the night around me, wondering when it would be our turn.

Finally, I could stand and went to each man, telling him what Wicker had told me, especially to stay alert. Not long after that, Elvis whispered that the line was moving, and we trudged forward again. We changed direction, starting up a hill at an angle to the slope.

At about 0300, rain started. First, occasional big drops slapped the leaves as they plummeted to the ground, but steadily the rain got harder and louder. It also got colder. Scared though we were, that was infantrymen's weather. The sound of the rain covered the sounds we were making, so we could move faster. Already soaked by the sweat of our exertion, we didn't mind the rain. But the cold added to our misery.

Just before 0400 we stopped again. After a few minutes, word came back that it would be another long stop. Tusi got the gun in position, and Harrington went down on his left. I checked on Elvis before standing behind the gun. I wanted to go down on my belly beside the other men so I could lay side-by-side with them and share their body heat. I was tired, so anything I did to try to relieve my discomfort would just make me prone to fall asleep. So I stood.

At 0430, I checked the luminous hands of my watch yet again. I wondered what was going on. I was surprised Wicker hadn't come back to talk to us. I made my way to where I thought I'd left Elvis. No one challenged me with a hushed query, so I whispered, "Elvis?"

He didn't answer so I tried twice more, raising my voice each time. There was still no answer. It's easy to lose your orientation in the jungle at night, so my first thought was that I hadn't gone far enough. I tried to take another step, but my foot drove into something soft. I knew it was a man's body, and I dropped to my knees. It was Elvis, and he grunted and sat up as I came down. Face-to-face, I demanded, "You fall asleep?"

"No!"

"You lyin' piece of shit!"

I was livid, but my first concern was to make sure we hadn't been left behind. "Where's the man in front of you?"

Elvis stumbled to his feet. He was mumbling and rotating in different directions. After having been asleep and in the darkness and the rain, he didn't even know which way we'd been headed.

"You dumb fuck!"

I shoved Elvis out of my way and went past him. I took exactly five steps and stopped. I heard nothing except the rain. "Wicker?" I called.

"Lee was in front of me," Elvis whispered over my shoulder.

"Lee? Lee!" I demanded.

There was no answer and I wondered if Lee also might have gone to sleep. I raised my voice and tried again. I took five more steps and tried it all once more. When there was still no answer, I turned and asked, "How far apart were you staying?"

"Ten ... yeah, ten feet."

I'd already gone that far, but I took five more steps and called for Lee and then Wicker. There was no answer. I knew we'd lost contact with the rest of the platoon and been left behind.

"Follow me back." I led Elvis to where my other three men waited, diligently doing their jobs, oblivious to the fact that we were now on our own. I stopped and tried to think my way out of the situation. It was bad, but I didn't panic. I was going to get my ass chewed for letting it happen, but I hoped that would be the worst of it. I jerked Elvis to my face. "Either we're going to die out here or you're going to get the shit beat out of you when we get back!"

I knelt down beside the three men huddled near the machine gun. "Hey. Listen up." I heard all three turn to look at me. I went on, trying to sound confident things would work out. "We got a break in contact—"

"Where? How far up?" asked Harrington.

I let out a breath. "Elvis fell asleep and—"

"That son of a bitch!"

Harrington started to get up. I knew they were all thinking the same thing.
"At ease! Stop!" I said. Harrington froze and I hurried on. "Okay? We're going to stay here for right now, and maybe they'll come back and get us." I knew it was a fantasy. With breaks in contact, the front of the platoon never knows they've lost the back until later. By then they've gone too far to retrace their steps, which at night may mean only fifty meters. And when a break was reported up the chain of command, permission to spend time looking for us would probably be denied since the rest of the platoon had a mission.

Since we got ourselves into this mess, it was up to us to get ourselves out of it. That was the ethic.

For a moment after I'd spoken there was no sound other than the rain. Then Harrington said, "Elvis, you hear me?"

"Yeah."

"Motherfucker. If we get out of this, you're dead."

No one said anything for a long time after. We just waited and listened. There was no point in trying to find the platoon in the dark, and I didn't want to get shot creeping up on them. The best thing to do was wait for sunrise. Since we knew the battalion was going to be pulled out of the area late in the afternoon of the coming day, we were in a jam. I doubted they'd leave us behind, but I wasn't sure. I was also aware this was the first time I'd be in charge of my team, these men, in this kind of situation. It's easy to control men when things go well, but this was not going well.

The rain didn't slow, but the blackness faded to gray. We watched up the trail, hoping someone would come back for us, but there was nothing. Poorly defined shadows emerged that seemed more a feature of the night than of any day. When it was light enough to see, Tusi, Harrington, and Oltin all took turns staring down Elvis. He kept looking at them, hoping for forgiveness, but each time all he saw were angry glares forcing him to turn away. I think that's when Elvis began to realize how far from home the jungles of Vietnam and death were.

I pulled out my map. I figured we had two options. We could try to follow the platoon in the hope of catching up, or we could head straight for the battalion's firebase. Tracking the platoon would be hard and slow because we'd be trying to avoid the enemy and stay on the platoon's trail, but not walk up on them so fast they'd shoot us by mistake. Going straight to the firebase would be easier inasmuch as I knew exactly where it was. But that idea was also very dangerous. Without a radio to tell them we were coming, we'd have to figure out how to get back into our battalion's perimeter without getting shot or shredded by a Claymore. Still, going to the firebase seemed like the better option.

Either way we went, I hoped we wouldn't stumble across the NVA. If we did, our little five-man team would last only minutes. We would just disappear into the jungle, and our families would never know what had happened to us. We would be names on a roll of Missing In Action.

I pulled the men together and explained the situation the way I saw it. "So we're going straight to the firebase," I concluded. No one said anything. They looked either at me or the map I held. "Let's go," I said.

Tusi and Oltin nodded.

Harrington hissed, "Yeah, and that stupid prick," he said, pointing at Elvis, "can walk point when we get close. Maybe they'll blow him away and save us the trouble."

"Shut up. I said we'll deal with him later."

An explosion in the distance was followed by sustained bursts of small-arms fire, which built in volume over several seconds.

"Ambush," Harrington whispered as we all stared through the trees.

"Oh, man," Oltin whined, turning to Elvis. "This is all your fault, man!"

I leaned in to the middle of them and said, "Shut up! Shut up! No more about Elvis! He fucked up. We all know that. We gotta get to the firebase before we worry about him. Got it?"

The firing in the distance continued as I spoke. The sound of one machine gun interrupted the faster, quieter clattering of M16s. We all knew it was our platoon in contact. Otherwise, we would have heard two machine guns firing. Tusi, cradling his M60 across his chest, looked at it and then at me. I knew what he was thinking. We should have been with them. But I shook my head. The fight would long be over before we got there, and we'd probably get shot by the Vietnamese and our own troops as we got close. Tusi's shoulders seemed to sag for an instant, but he nodded his agreement.

There were loud detonations as our platoon called in artillery or mortar fire. After about twenty explosions, the small-arms firing stopped.

"Let's go," I said again. "Harrington, you're on point. I'm behind you. Tusi and Oltin, you're behind me. Elvis, you're trail and rear guard." Leaning toward him, I said, "And, so help me God, if you lose contact with us, we're not going to come looking for you. Now," I said glancing at each man in turn, "Let's go."

The men stood and got ready to move as I opened my compass and compared it to the map. I confirmed the direction and pointed. Harrington nodded and stood. Walking cautiously, he pushed between the trees and twisted past the thorny vines that scratched our skin.

We walked for hours. Around noon, we came across a small and poorly defined trail. It was probably used by locals as a path between two of the widely dispersed villages in the area. After some hesitation, we decided to take it as long as it continued the way we wanted to go. We did not often use existing trails, preferring to cut our own. If you stayed on an existing trail long enough, the Viet Cong or NVA regulars would ambush you. I thought the risk worth taking this time. As we started moving again, two helicopters rushed over us, just feet above the trees. We saw the red crosses on the doors. Medevacs.

Though the rain continued, we heard no sounds of battle. By early afternoon, we knew we were getting close to our firebase. We came across a small stream. It was swollen. Its water splashed white as it pounded from rock to rock in the little valley it had etched as it ran to the low ground. We stopped to fill our canteens. While the rest of the men worked in silence, holding their green plastic jugs under the water, I checked my map and compass.

"How far?" Harrington whispered.

"About a klick."

Harrington nodded and turned away. The other men waited as I put away my map and went to work filling my canteens. I filled the first one, then I dropped in three of the iodine tablets we used to purify the foul water. I screwed the top back on and put it away. When I reached for my second canteen, I sensed something was wrong and looked up.

Tusi was staring across the small stream. He held his right hand flat, palm to the ground, slowly moving it up and down. The other men were going to their knees as I put my canteen down in the mud and pulled up my M16. The rain splattered around us in the green gloom as we waited for Tusi to tell us what was wrong.

Tusi pulled the machine gun tighter against his side, its black strap over his back and shoulder, and wrapped his right hand around the black pistol grip. I heard him click off the safety. I looked away from him and tried to see into the vegetation. I saw nothing and began moving my head slightly from side to side, straining to see farther into the tangle of undergrowth on the other side of the stream.

"What?" I finally whispered.

Tusi looked at me with an expression that said he didn't understand why I couldn't see what was obvious to him. Then he turned and stepped into some bushes that extended into the stream. I watched his foot disappear under the water and waited as he moved it around, feeling for a place where it wouldn't slip. Then he brought his other foot into the rushing water before lowering himself to a squat in the middle of the flooded undergrowth. Water swirled around his muscular thighs as he stared at the spot where the trail emerged on the far side of the stream. He waved me forward.

I stepped into the water and knelt beside him after glancing up to make sure no one was above us. When I lowered my eyes, he was pointing the barrel of the black machine gun at several indentations in the mud where the trail exited the water. They were overlapping prints of sandal-clad feet. The rainwater was running down the trail, cascading from one print to the next, erasing them.

"Watering detail," I said.

"We just missed 'em," he answered.

"They just missed us."

We knew that where there were a few enemy soldiers on a watering detail, there were many, many more.

I turned to Harrington. "Let's go! Up the stream! Move!"

Harrington stepped past me. He glanced at the prints and began working up the streambed. I scooped up the canteen I'd dropped. Without filling it, I rammed it into my belt. I followed Harrington and made sure Tusi was close behind me. After twenty steps, I turned and saw the bobbing heads of Oltin and Elvis behind Tusi.

After ten minutes of moving quickly, I pushed my hand into Harrington's back. He turned. I pointed for him to leave the stream that was diminishing in size as we approached the top of the ridge. He led us out of the gully, and we all came together in an area of thin brush. I knew we were close to our battalion's firebase, but I wanted to check my map because we'd veered off the specific approach I'd chosen. We were soaked, and red mud streaked our pant legs.

"How far?" Oltin asked, his cheeks billowing out.

I ignored the question and whispered, "Everybody face out." Doing as told, the four men made a circle, their backs to me, each man's weapon and eyes moving together as they searched the surrounding vegetation for approaching enemy soldiers.

After looking at my map and compass, I pointed. "Should be about four hundred meters that way."

Tusi checked which way I indicated and then looked through the brush.

"What were they doing up here?" Oltin asked.

I looked at Oltin and then Tusi. It was so obvious to me, as I was sure it was to Tusi and Harrington.

"They're going to attack our battalion as it pulls out," Tusi said.

As he finished speaking, I heard a helicopter approaching. Through the branches, we caught glimpses of the big, twin-engine Chinook as it hovered over our firebase. After thirty seconds, it rose straight up, lifting one of the 105 artillery pieces off the hilltop. Slung beneath the powerful chopper, the howitzer swung gently as the Shit Hook continued to turn and climb.

Not only had the withdrawal begun, but I also knew our company would be returning to the firebase soon. Battalion would not pull the artillery tubes unless the patrols still out could get fire support from the very limited-range mortars that were also in the firebase.

I glanced around. My men were all staring at me. We were on the outside, isolated in a no-man's land bristling with weapons.

Part 5: A Short Distance

We wove through the brush as we approached the battalion's hilltop perimeter, desperate not to make any sounds that would give us away to the nearby NVA soldiers. Now on higher ground, the vegetation was not as thick and we could see farther.

Harrington stopped and slowly went to his knees. I leaned against his back and looked over his shoulder. "What?"

He raised his hand. I sighted along his arm and spotted a handful of NVA soldiers quietly digging in two mortars pointed at our firebase. My mouth got dry and my heart sped up, but I turned to the men behind me. I put my finger to my compressed lips. Then I made my hand into a gun, as a child might do playing cowboys and Indians. Turning it upside down, I pointed toward the NVA soldiers. The hand signal meant "enemy."

"This is bad!" Harrington whispered.

"Shh ... move away. Drop down below the ridge until we're out of sight, then turn back to the firebase."

He nodded and we started moving as another helicopter came in and plucked a second howitzer from the hilltop. After ten minutes, Harrington stopped and again went to his knees. He pointed. About thirty meters away, I saw three NVA soldiers crawling forward to a position from which to fire on our battalion's perimeter. My stomach was very tight, but I ignored it and put my hand on his shoulder. I pointed down the ridge and then back to the firebase. I hoped we could find a gap in their lines.

Harrington again changed direction. After twenty more meters, while we were still headed down the slope, he stopped and raised his arm. "Fuckers are everywhere!"

I stuck my head next to his.

Looking to where he pointed, I saw a line of NVA soldiers about forty meters away, their backs to us, focusing on another ridgeline beyond and below the one on which they waited. They were watching the ridgeline by which we'd left the firebase days earlier. The enemy soldiers were betting our company would return to the perimeter the same way we'd gone out.

It was also obvious they were setting up a coordinated attack. The NVA unit was going to hit our returning company at the same time they attacked the firebase, which would be concurrent with our battalion's ongoing withdrawal. They had an almost perfect plan to attack us at the most confusing time.

The rest of the men bunched up behind me, and Oltin whined, "Oh, Jesus, man!"

"Shut up!"

"What're we—"

I slapped my hand over Oltin's mouth and hissed, "Shh!" Then, "Everyone, back ..." I looked around and saw a thick stand of trees and underbrush. "Back there. Move!"

We made our way into the trees until I was sure we were out of sight. I had everyone put their heads together so they could hear me. My voice was shaking and high, but they paid close attention. "Listen up. This is what we're going to do. Okay? We're going to attack the NVA that are down here ... the ones that are going to ambush our company. We'll use our Claymores to blow away those guys setting up the ambush. We pull the fuses and drop them. Then we sneak up behind those three enemy we saw on the perimeter. We kill them and then run into our firebase."

"How the fuck are we going to keep the guys in the firebase from shooting us?" Harrington blurted.

"Hopefully they'll figure out who we are."

He kept staring, his mouth hanging open. "We're just gonna have to get lucky," I said.

"Luck my ass—"

"You got a better idea?" I demanded, leaning closer to him. There were too many NVA soldiers around to waste time arguing.

Harrington looked at Tusi, who said nothing, then at Elvis before turning back to me. Tusi quietly put his M60 on the ground and pulled the carrying strap over his head so he could get his Claymore.

"This is fucked up, man," Oltin said, trying to convince the others that there had to be a better way.

Harrington relented and swung his rucksack around so he could pull out his Claymore.

"Fuck," Oltin swore before pulling off his rucksack.

When everyone had their Claymore in hand and had put their rucks on, we stood and stepped out of the thicket, moving toward the NVA's ambush line. The rain got harder as we crept forward, but we heard another Chinook coming in to hover above the firebase.

I directed Harrington to a small knoll above the NVA soldiers. Once there, I turned and nodded. We spread out so there were a few meters between us. I bent and shoved the Claymore's metal supports into the ground. Then I rotated it on its hinged legs until it pointed down the slope at the unsuspecting enemy soldiers. On either side of me, the four men on my team did the same thing. Due to the slope of the land, the distance, and all the intervening trees, we'd probably do the NVA little real damage. The enemy soldiers closest to us would die. The main thing, however, was to warn the men in the firebase and preempt the NVA attack so we could use the confusion to enter the perimeter.

Kneeling behind my Claymore, I looked left and then right. I held the fuse igniter in my hand. It was a thing about the size of a cigar with a pull-ring on one end. Everyone looked at me and I could tell they were ready, though scared. I looped my finger through the pull-ring and took a deep breath. Once we ignited the fuses, we had two minutes before we would begin fighting our way through the enemy soldiers surrounding our base. I remember thinking some if not all of us would be dead within three minutes.

I looked down and pulled the ring. There was a slight pop followed by four identical sounds as the other men ignited their fuses. I held the fuse igniter for a moment. A wisp of smoke curled out of it before I spread my fingers. It fell out of my hand and bounced on the wet ground. Just below the fuse igniter, the fuse's casing turned black as the flame that would ignite the blasting cap and the Claymore burned inside it.

"Let's go!" I whispered. I stood and pulled my M16 around. With my right thumb, I pushed the selector lever to "AUTO."

Harrington stood and headed back up the ridge. We hurried along the route we'd used earlier. He stopped and looked for the three NVA soldiers we'd seen crawling into position. After looking over his shoulder about ten seconds, I asked, "See 'em?"

"No!"

I looked through the nearby vegetation to our battalion's firebase beyond. I checked my watch. About fifteen seconds of our two minutes remained. "Fuck it! Just go! Go!"

Harrington started moving, bent at the waist with his M16 in front of him, walking quickly toward the perimeter, still trying to minimize how much noise we were making.

The first Claymore exploded with a loud, single crack. There were screams, then yelling, and we began to run. Next to the trail in front of Harrington, vegetation rustled as a camouflaged NVA soldier rolled to his back, looking up at us. We both fired and the enemy soldier's body jerked with the impact of the bullets.

Two more of the Claymores exploded seconds apart. Tree bark hit me in the face as a machine gunner from our firebase shot at us, slamming his bullets into a tree near me. We all dropped but kept crawling toward the perimeter. The volume of fire coming out from the firebase increased as more men got their weapons into operation. I'm sure they didn't know what they were firing at, but they were pumping out rounds.

A bullet ricocheted off something and hit Oltin in the side. It drove him down and sideways, but did not penetrate his flak jacket. He rolled to his back, mouth open and face white.

Tusi's machine gun began hammering out rounds. I turned and saw him, kneeling on the ground, waving the big gun back and forth as he fired into the vegetation on our left. His entire body shook as the M60 banged out bullet after bullet. The big gun sucked the shiny brass rounds into its left side and spit the empty shells and black metal links out its right side.

I spotted a depression in the ground ahead, possibly an old bomb crater. I pointed at the hole. "Keep going!"

Harrington crawled toward it and I turned to make sure the other men were following. Tusi continued to fire, so I grabbed Elvis's arm and shoved him past me. Then Tusi followed, running with a short belt of ammo swinging from the left side of the gun.

A swarm of bullets came at us from the direction Tusi had been firing. I managed to jerk two fragmentation grenades off my belt. I pulled the pins and threw them toward the source of the firing. As they exploded, Tusi ran by me, stumbling in a crouched run, steam curling off his machine gun's black barrel. I hoped the explosions would create confusion and the enemy would lose track of us.

I was the last man to jump in the hole. The sound of firing near us ebbed, though it was louder farther up the hill.

A young NVA soldier smashed out of the vegetation and ran into the depression close beside me.

For half a second, we all looked at him as his eyes raced across each of us, his eyes big and mouth open. Then, instead of using his weapon, he turned and tried to get out of the crater. Harrington and Tusi rotated their weapons. "No!" I was afraid more firing would give away our hiding place. I dropped my M16 and pulled out the big knife I carried as I dove after the enemy soldier. I tackled the kid, dragging him down into the mud and brush. He rolled to his back, looking up at me, his helmet falling off. He shouted something at me and tried to knock my hands away. I struggled to get my left hand over his mouth as I straddled his stomach.

The first time I tried to drive the knife into him I didn't know what I was doing. I'd never killed anything with a knife before. I hit his cheekbone and slammed the knife into the ground beside him. He paused for half a second before slapping at my face again.

I remember being furious. I'd never been so mad. I just wanted him to shut up. I didn't want to kill him like that, but I pulled the knife out of the ground and tried to stab him with it again. I thought I needed to drive the knife as I'd drive my fist in a fight, and the point of the knife went deep into his left eye. But it was too big to go through his eye socket and into his brain.

He screamed and put his hands to his face. The kid stopped slapping at me, and his shouting sounded more like pleading. He knew it was over. And I suddenly realized I had to think about what to do with a knife to kill a man.

With my left hand I pushed his face back, exposing his neck, and then I drove the knife deep into his throat, just below his Adam's apple, driving the point into his chest. I leaned over the knife, using my weight to push it as far into him as I could. I felt the tip of my knife getting hung up on his vertebra.

Oltin landed beside me, dropping to his knees and bringing the butt of his M16 down hard on the kid's face. The enemy soldier stopped screaming as I rolled off him, pulling my knife out of his chest, but he wasn't dead. He still bounced on the ground, gurgling blood with his arms out to his sides, his fingers digging in the mud.

It was very hard to stand, so Tusi and Oltin helped me get on my feet and pick up my M16. I kept looking at the dying kid until Tusi jerked me to the other side of the crater. That's when I realized it had been silent, but then I could hear all the firing again, and I could hear Oltin talking to me, but I could not make sense of his words. As I tried to understand what he was saying, Elvis looked up at me, eyes huge. He was motionless.

One of the Claymores on our perimeter exploded, which helped clear my head. We instinctively ducked as the steel bearings ripped bark from trees and stripped off leaves. Bullets from the opposite direction were slamming into tree trunks around us.

"What're we gonna do?" Oltin demanded.

I looked at the line of bunkers across the bullet-swept no-man's land. It seemed such a short distance, but so far away we'd never reach it. I could see the black slits and yellow flame flashing out of the fighting positions as our friends fired toward us. In the cataclysm of shooting, explosions, and screaming, I couldn't think of anything except that I wanted to be on the other side of the firing line. Before, getting everyone back to safety was a task, a mission. Now it was something I wanted for me. I wanted to go home. I wanted us all to go home. But I didn't know how to get close enough to the perimeter to tell them to let us in without getting shot. I didn't think they'd be able to hear us yelling over the roar of the surrounding battle.

I was petrified, and I didn't know what to do. I've never forgotten that feeling of being unable to help my men. Without having to look at them, I felt their stares, and I couldn't move. I was failing them.

Elvis jumped out of the depression. Tusi tried to grab him, but he missed. Elvis ran toward our firebase. When he got out of the trees, he began yelling and waving his M16 over his head. He screamed, "Hey! We're American! Hey, HEY! Help us! We're from Bravo Company!"

We all hesitated. Then Harrington and Oltin began to shout at our men in the firebase. Tusi turned to me and grabbed the red smoke grenade I'd strapped to my gear. He pulled the pin and threw it behind us. It was a good idea. The men on the perimeter might see the red smoke and pause long enough to recognize Elvis as an American.

Elvis kept running forward, shouting his message.

"They're slowing down!" Harrington screamed as the red smoke cloud began to billow behind us. There were fewer muzzle flashes from American weapons, but there were even more bullets slapping around us as the NVA targeted the red smoke.

As we watched Elvis, his right arm jerked out and away from his body, hard, with a viciously unnatural movement. He fell sideways, pulled by the momentum of the bullet that had shattered his forearm, dropping his M16.

All of us in the hole instinctively leaned forward.

Elvis collapsed to his back, his helmet rolling off. He inspected his lower arm and we could see the blood squirting out of the shattered area above the wrist. He rocked back and forth on his back a few times, and then he twisted to his knees. Elvis reached for his M16 with his left hand. Dragging the weapon, he began to crawl toward the perimeter. He held his right arm to his side. We could see the blood falling off it in thick drops. He started shouting again, but his voice was not as loud and his words came slowly.

I grabbed Harrington by the shoulder and shouted, "Come on!" As we struggled out of the crater, I turned to Tusi and Oltin and screamed, "Cover us and then come!"

Harrington and I ran for Elvis. We tripped and stumbled over the rough ground, but were quickly at his side. I grabbed his right shoulder with my left hand and jerked him to his feet. Harrington grasped his left arm and we started toward the perimeter. I looked up and saw some of the men on the perimeter crawling out of their bunkers. They were also yelling and waving, trying to get their buddies not to fire at us.

Tusi's machine gun stopped, but I couldn't look to see if he was following us. In front of me, two men struggled out of their position and ran toward us. One was a black man in a flak jacket and a brown Army T-shirt with the sleeves cut off. The other was a tall white guy with blond hair wearing just his T-shirt and a dark green bandanna around his head. I can still see him gritting his teeth as he ran to help us. Both men left their weapons behind.

They reached us and I pushed Elvis at them before spinning and dropping to a crouch to check on Tusi and Oltin. Both were running toward us as fast as they could. The shiny belt of ammunition hanging out of Tusi's gun swung in rhythm to his steps.

Though I didn't have a target, I raised my weapon and aimed past Tusi. I fired into the tangle of green vegetation in the hopes of getting us the last seconds we needed to reach safety. I emptied my magazine just as Tusi and Oltin went by me. I ran after them.

I saw that more men had come out to help us. Two carried the tall soldier with blond hair. He'd been shot. He hung between the soldiers carrying him, head down and feet dragging in the mud, blood blackening his left side.

We made it into the firebase's perimeter but kept running until we were well beyond the outer bunkers. An officer, a captain, grabbed me and yelled, "What happened?"

I swallowed hard, then yelled over the firing, "The NVA are circling us! They were going to ambush our company ..."

"How many?"

"We saw maybe forty, fifty of 'em ... and two mortars where we came in!"

The firing continued around us. "Where're their mortars?" He shouted, pushing a map at me. "Show me!" Then, over the roar of weapons going off around us, he ordered, "Follow me to the CP!"

I nodded. He turned and ran in a crouch toward the command bunker. I impulsively realized I'd rather be with my men, and I'd already told him everything I knew. I turned and went the opposite direction, looking for my team.

Part 6: Driving in Darkness

The NVA attack was confused and uncoordinated because of what we'd done. The battalion's withdrawal stopped, and our company was told to hold their position and go into a defensive position where they were. For the rest of the night, artillery pounded the entire area, except for our battalion firebase and the spot where our company had stopped. There'd been only one death: the blond man I'd given Elvis to when we were running for the perimeter. We got Elvis to the medic's tent, where they kept him until they medevaced him out the next morning, after the NVA had left the area.

I don't remember much about what happened over the next week, other than we went back to our basecamp for a few days and then back into the bush. We were part of a big battalion air-assault operation, again along the Cambodian border west of Dak To.

As we came into the landing zone, we took a lot of fire. Another Huey flew beside us but about ten meters back, so I was only thirty meters from its cockpit. About twenty meters above the ground, I saw a huge splash of red as the pilot in the other bird got shot from the far side, probably in his head. Blood washed all over the inside of the windscreen. I don't know why the copilot could not control the chopper, or if he was also dead, but the Huey's nose dived toward the dirt, men jumping out from much too high. Its rotor shattered when it clipped the ground, before it landed upsidedown. Pieces of the broken blade flew through our chopper, one piece nicking my shoulder.

The downed chopper's rotor was still spinning, making the chopper bounce up and down, and its tail boom tried to rotate in the opposite direction. The craft was disintegrating, pieces flying off as it hopped across the ground, pounding on some of the men who had jumped out seconds earlier.

Our pilot jerked his Huey sideways as I was about to jump off the skid. I slipped and came down hard on my lower back. I had landed on a large rock and couldn't move my legs. Bullets were chipping the rocks around me as I rolled to the dirt.

I remember lying there, trying to get my rucksack off to hide behind and get my M16 ready. But I was afraid if I moved too much I'd just hurt myself worse. So I lay there staring at the blue sky, watching three more waves of Hueys descending into that LZ, and listening to engines whining, men screaming, and weapons firing. I was again unable to help my men.

After about twenty minutes we had enough soldiers there we could enlarge the LZ, and then the medevacs started coming in to get all the wounded. They medevaced me on the first bird as the LZ was still taking fire. On a stretcher in the Huey's bay, I wondered if I'd ever see my men again—or walk again. I watched small holes opening in the helicopter's skin as the enemy bullets went through it. I remember the relief I felt once we reached altitude. I don't remember being in pain, so I wiped away the tears before the medics could see them.

They sent me to a hospital in Japan, where a week later I saw the flow of casualties from the enemy's Tet Offensive. Most of them were Marines from the meat grinder of Hue. They were angry. Shortly afterward, the Army sent me back to the States.

I spent three months in Letterman Army Hospital. The damage wasn't permanent—at least not to my back—and my recovery went well. Now I can do almost anything anyone else can do at my age. They gave me a medical discharge and disability pay for life, and I went on to college but could no longer stand the idea of teaching. I got an accounting degree instead. I prefer working with numbers to working with people.

Tusi made sergeant and became a squad leader before he left Vietnam. He stayed in for twenty-seven years.

Oltin did his tour and went home and I've not heard of him since.

Harrington got out and bounced around for a while. He finally became a mechanic and now owns a shop in Durham, Michigan.

Elvis went home after he was shot, his right arm half an inch shorter than his left, and he spent the remainder of his enlistment stationed at Fort Ord, California. He did go back to school, in Boulder. He now teaches scriptwriting in the film and theater department of Florida State University. He's written several plays that were produced locally and has published two novels. The second one sold well, I think. He told me the titles and I meant to get them, but I never have.

Wicker survived Vietnam but died in a car wreck in 1973. He was a company first sergeant at the time and left a wife and two little girls. I met them at his funeral.

Before he died, Wicker worked hard at keeping us all in contact. We even had the "First Annual Second Squad Reunion" in Denver in 1972. As luck would have it, several of us lived nearby at the time. After I'd gotten out, I went to school in Wyoming while Elvis was in school in Boulder. Several of the men, including Wicker, were stationed at Fort Carson, south of Denver. A few other guys had ended up at Fort Riley, in Kansas. One more was stationed at Fort Hood, not far from Dallas. Another fellow who'd gotten out lived in Salt Lake City. In all, twelve men showed up at the reunion. I didn't know most of them since my stay in the squad had been so short.

At the reunion, I returned Elvis's diary to him. Several times between 1968 and 1972, I reread what he'd written in those few days he and I were in Vietnam together. I was curious about his perceptions of what went on there and what he thought about the war. And his opinions of me.

It was a strange moment when I handed his diary back to him. He reached for it with his right hand, and I could see the scars above his wrist. He'd been shot risking his life to save us when I was unable to move.

He took the diary from me and stared at it with furrowed brows. Neither one of us spoke. Then he nodded before looking at me, and I shrugged. Neither one of us knew what to say.

As we stood there, one of the guys who'd joined the squad after Tet walked up. Neither of us knew him. He asked about our time there and if we'd served together. We nodded but didn't speak.

Elvis and I sat at opposite ends of the table for dinner that night. There was a lot of Jim Beam whiskey and smoking, but I don't remember much of it. I do remember I felt out of place, and trying to talk felt awkward. I did not drink much and left early without saying goodbye to Wicker, which I later regretted. It was the last time I saw him.

I drove much of the night to get home. I went through Boulder on my way. I assume Elvis was in his car, in the darkness, not far behind me as he headed home.

Elvis had seen it all differently, as something both primeval and essential to the way men grow and learn to live together.

Every time I'd reread his words before I gave his diary back to him, I'd come to a place where a page was missing—one I'd ripped out and forced him to eat. I don't like thinking about what I made him do, even though it was necessary. It was my job to keep him alive. I hadn't thought Elvis was ready for Vietnam. He didn't understand it. But I wasn't ready for Vietnam, either, even though I thought I understood it. I came to believe neither one of us had been ready for what waited for us in those jungles, and we both left our youth there. It died in Vietnam.

Elvis and I have made a halfhearted attempt to stay in touch. We trade Christmas cards. And they always arrive late, usually near the end of January, about the time of Tet in Vietnam.

Endnotes

Thank you. I hope you enjoyed this story and found it engaging.

Please write me directly at SaltLake62@gmal.com with any comments or feedback. I look forward to hearing from you.

And please write a short review at Amazon or your other favorite site. Let other people know what you thought of it. If you would, write it now while the story is still fresh in your mind. I look forward to seeing your review and otherwise hearing from you. Thank you!

If you would like to see more of my work, you can read an excerpt from my upcoming novel, Lonely Hunter, at my website.

A. L. Tiffany

Acknowledgements

Though writing is a uniquely solitary endeavor, bringing a novel to market takes a team. I want to thank a few people for their help in getting this story written, polished, and published.

As always, my wife provided invaluable feedback on the story and the telling. She finds time to go through everything I ask her to review. She's also a partner and best friend, and together we've learned about life, which has helped me greatly as a writer. And when I was away for extended periods of time in my role as a soldier, she managed our home and four children. It has often been a lonely and challenging task.

Speaking of my children: I want to thank my older daughters for their help. They know little of the Vietnam War other than that their Grandfather served there, and that we flew over it a few times when we lived in Asia. Between them, though, they have assisted with the artwork and been surprisingly helpful reviewers. Natasha gets special thanks for her help with the cover artwork and the work she did creating the map.

I'd also like to thank my anonymous reviewers at the online writing workshop, www.CritiqueCircle.com. It's a fantastic resource for writers at all levels to submit their work and get critiques from a thoughtful and accomplished group of readers and writers. Their feedback has been insightful and rigorous, which has been hugely helpful.

Another "thank you" goes out to the team at The Editorial Department (www.editorialdepartment.com) for their help, and the professional editing done by Julie Miller. Julie's sharp eye and insights have been invaluable. Jane Ryder also shared her perceptions that helped me understand how to better write the story I wanted to share.

About the Author

Allen Tiffany is a retired Army Infantry Officer and has graduated from the Army's Airborne and Ranger schools and the Command and General Staff College. He has also earned his graduate degree in Creative Writing from the University of Kansas and has published a number of professional articles, a short story, has been a newspaper columnist, and he has been a fiction editor for a campus literature magazine. Allen was born in Kansas and has lived in Georgia, California, Texas and Singapore. When he is not working in the high-tech industry, he spends his time with his wife and four daughters or writing. He also enjoys long distance biking.

Made in the USA
Middletown, DE
05 September 2017